FIR IY

SUPER
SANDCASTLE
State Stories

MONTY'S ICE PICK

~ A Story About Alaska ~

Written by Katherine Hengel

Illustrated by Bob Doucet

Consulting Editor, Diane Craig, M.A./Reading Specialist

ABDO
Publishing Company

Published by ABDO Publishing Company
8000 West 78th Street, Edina, Minnesota 55439.

Printed in the United States of America, North Mankato, Minnesota
112009
012010

 PRINTED ON RECYCLED PAPER

Editor: Katherine Hengel
Content Developer: Nancy Tuminelly
Cover and Interior Design: Anders Hanson, Mighty Media
Production: Colleen Dolphin, Mighty Media
Photo Credits: Floyd Davidson, One Mile Up, Shutterstock,
Shana Zaiser. Quarter-dollar coin image from the United States Mint

Library of Congress Cataloging-in-Publication Data

Hengel, Katherine.
  Monty's ice pick : a story about Alaska / Katherine Hengel ;
illustrated by Bob Doucet.
    p. cm. -- (Fact & fable: state stories)
  ISBN 978-1-60453-925-7
  1. Alaska--Juvenile literature. I. Doucet, Bob, ill. II. Title.
  F904.3.H455 2010
  979.8--dc22

                              2009033399

Super SandCastle™ books are created by a team of professional
educators, reading specialists, and content developers around
five essential components—phonemic awareness, phonics,
vocabulary, text comprehension, and fluency—to assist young
readers as they develop reading skills and strategies and
increase their general knowledge. All books are written,
reviewed, and leveled for guided reading, early reading
intervention, and Accelerated Reader® programs for use in
shared, guided, and independent reading and writing activities
to support a balanced approach to literacy instruction.

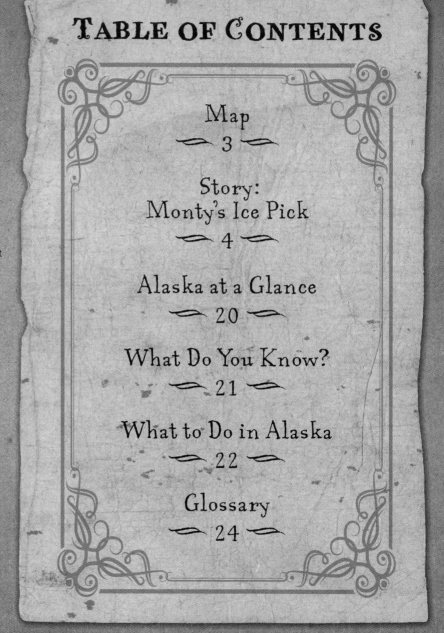

TABLE OF CONTENTS

bowhead whale
(pg. 17)

bush flying
(pg. 13)

Gates of the Arctic
National Park
(pg. 18)

Bering Strait
(pg. 16)

Nome

Fairbanks

ALASKA

willow
ptarmigan
(pg. 7)

Bethel

Talkeetna   Valdez

Iditarod Trail
Sled Dog Race
(pg. 11)

Anchorage

Skagway

moose
(pg. 5)

Seward

Homer

Glacier Bay
National Park
(pg. 6)

Juneau
(pg. 4)

Ketchikan

LEGEND

CAPITAL   STORY START

CITY   STORY PATH

MOUNTAINS

RIVER   STORY END

Juneau

Juneau is the capital of Alaska. It was named after gold **prospector** Joe Juneau. Juneau is in the Alaskan **panhandle**. It is at the bottom of Mount Juneau.

MONTY'S ICE PICK

Monty the moose loves ice climbing. He climbs with his friends Morrie the mountain goat and Coco the coyote. They like to climb frozen waterfalls the best. They all belong to the Juneau Ice Climbing Club. Rizzo the bear is the club leader. She taught them all to be safe climbers. She knows all the best places in Juneau to climb!

Monty and his friends want to climb in Valdez.
But Monty's mom Miranda says it's **dangerous**.
She won't let him go unless she comes along.

"We'll leave early and see Glacier Bay together first,"
she says. "Then we'll meet your friends in Valdez."

"Great," Monty thinks to himself.

Moose

The moose is the state land **mammal** of Alaska. Male moose can weigh more than 1,300 pounds (590 kg)! Male moose grow huge antlers, which they **shed** in the winter. Their antlers grow back every spring. Female moose are very protective of their babies.

5

Glacier Bay National Park and Preserve

A glacier is a large, slow-moving piece of ice. There are sixteen glaciers in Glacier Bay National Park and Preserve. They start high in the snowy mountains and stretch down to the shore. Most of the freshwater on earth is in glaciers.

Monty makes sure he packs his favorite ice pick in his backpack. He might have to go to Valdez with his mom. But he won't go without his pick! Monty and his mom are thirsty when they get to Glacier Bay National Park. Monty sets his backpack on a bench. He follows his mom to get a drink of water.

When they return, Monty cries, "Oh, no! My backpack is gone!" He runs to the park office. He **describes** his backpack to Willow Ptarmigan, the park ranger.

"A team of sled dogs just left here. Maybe one of them grabbed it by accident," Willow says. "You might be able to catch them! They were on their way to the big race."

"Come on, Monty," Miranda says. "We're off to Anchorage."

Willow Ptarmigan

The state bird of Alaska is the willow ptarmigan. Ptarmigan is pronounced TAR-mi-gen. It is a **medium-sized** grouse that doesn't **migrate**.

Willow ptarmigan males help raise the young. They are the only kind of grouse that do that!

7

Monty doesn't care about anything in the backpack except for his pick. He'd still have it if his mom had let him go with his friends.

"Why are we going to Anchorage?" he asks as they hurry around the Gulf of Alaska.

"Because the sled dog that has your pack is going there," Miranda says.

Gulf of Alaska

The Gulf of Alaska is a part of the Pacific Ocean. Forests, mountains, and glaciers line the coast. Many storms begin in the Gulf of Alaska. They can turn into huge Alaskan snowstorms!

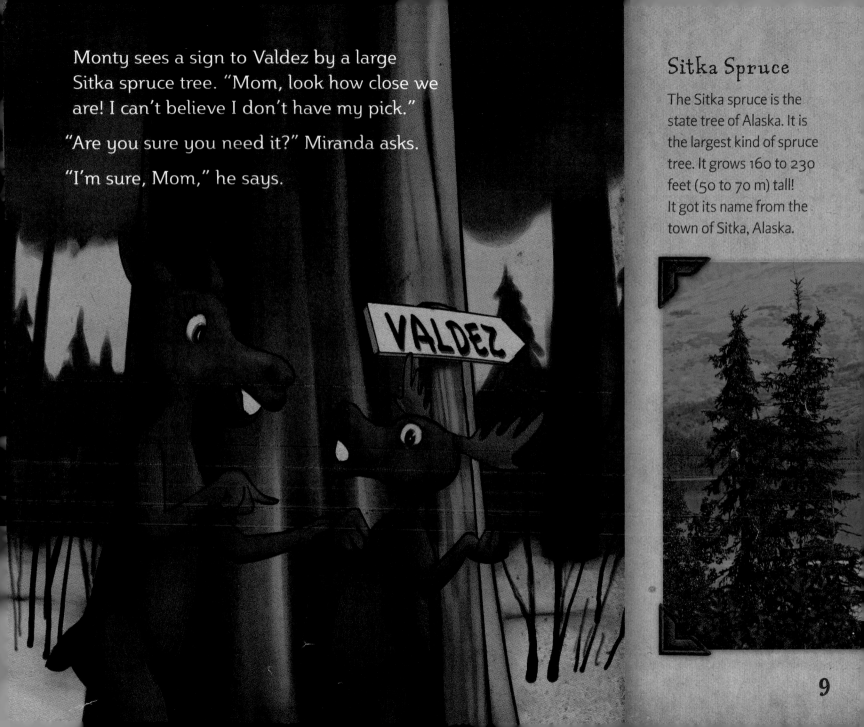

Monty sees a sign to Valdez by a large Sitka spruce tree. "Mom, look how close we are! I can't believe I don't have my pick."

"Are you sure you need it?" Miranda asks.

"I'm sure, Mom," he says.

Sitka Spruce

The Sitka spruce is the state tree of Alaska. It is the largest kind of spruce tree. It grows 160 to 230 feet (50 to 70 m) tall! It got its name from the town of Sitka, Alaska.

Anchorage

Almost half of the people in Alaska live in Anchorage! Anchorage got its start as the construction port for the Alaska Railroad. The railroad was built between 1915 and 1923.

There are people everywhere in Anchorage! But Monty and Miranda get there too late. The race has already started. "Now what?" Monty cries.

"We can meet the dogs at the finish line and get your pick back," Miranda says. "Or, we can meet your friends in Valdez tomorrow. I'm sure you could borrow an ice pick from Morrie or Coco."

Monty doesn't know what to do. "I want my pick back, Mom. But isn't this race more than a thousand miles long? How will we get to the finish line?"

"We won't be walking, Monty. I have friends here who can help us. Let's go!"

Iditarod Trail Sled Dog Race

The Iditarod Trail Sled Dog Race is held every year in Alaska. Each sled is pulled by a team of 16 sled dogs. The person driving a team is called a musher. The race begins near Anchorage and ends in Nome. The trail is more than 1150 miles (1850 km) long!

Monty follows his mother to a strange little shop called Four-Spot Flyers. It's right outside the city. Miranda says, "Baldy! It's been ages! I have to borrow one of your birds."

"Well if it isn't Miranda Moose, the best bush pilot in Alaska!" Baldy replies.

Now Monty is really confused. "What's the matter, son?" Baldy asks. "Didn't you know your mom moves like a dragonfly in the sky?"

Four-Spot Skimmer Dragonfly

The four-spot skimmer dragonfly is the state insect of Alaska. It can fly up to 35 miles per hour (56 kph)! It can also fly backward and make sharp turns. Skilled Alaskan bush pilots are often compared to four-spot skimmer dragonflies.

Baldy shows them to the plane. Monty's mom quickly prepares for takeoff. "I can't believe you know how to fly this thing!" Monty says.

Miranda grins and says, "It's as easy as Eskimo pie!"

Eskimo Pie

1 stick butter

15-ounce package Oreo®cookies, crushed

½ gallon of any ice cream

9-ounce carton Cool Whip®

Melt the butter. Mix in the crushed cookies. Put half of the mixture in the bottom of a pie pan. Mix the ice cream and Cool Whip® together. Spread the ice cream mixture on top of the cookies. Top with the rest of the cookie mixture. Put the pie in the freezer.

Bush Flying

Bush planes have special tires, floats, and skis. They can land just about anywhere! Bush planes don't need a lot of space to take off or land. Early bush pilots brought supplies to small villages in Alaska. There are many places in Alaska that can only be reached by plane.

13

Monty has never been in a plane before. He is **amazed**! He can see mountains and then the Yukon River.

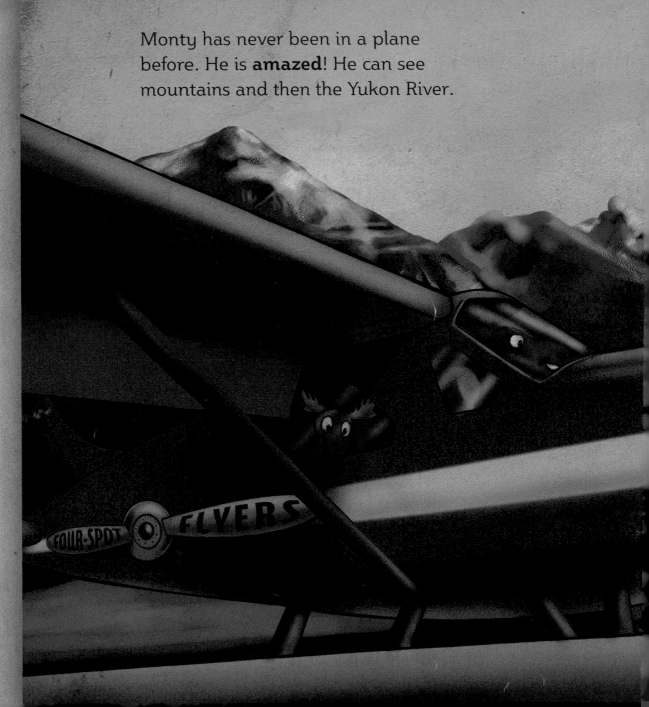

Yukon River

The Yukon River starts in Canada and flows all the way across Alaska. It ends at the Bering Sea. The river is 1,980 miles (3,186 km) long. It is the third-longest river in the United States.

Soon after that, Miranda lands the plane near Nome. That is where the sled dog race finishes. The sun is setting, and they are both tired. "This was actually a pretty cool day," Monty says.

Miranda smiles. "Tomorrow I'll show you the Bering Strait." Monty and Miranda fall fast asleep.

Nome

Nome is a port city on the Bering Sea. It is on the Seward Peninsula. Before European explorers came, only Eskimos lived in the area. Many people came to Nome in 1898 when gold was discovered.

Bering Strait

The Bering Strait is a small waterway between Asia and North America. It is 53 miles (85 km) wide. Many scientists believe that land used to connect the two continents. People and animals may have crossed between the two continents!

ASIA

Bering Strait

NORTH AMERICA

The next morning, they walk along the coast. Miranda tells Monty to look west. "This is the Bering Strait. It's only about 50 miles across," she says. "Many believe there was once land here."

Just then, a huge whale appears! "Is that you, Boris?" Miranda yells from the shore.

"Hi, Miranda! What brings you here?" Boris asks.

"It all started in Glacier Bay. My son lost something very important to him," Miranda explains.

But Monty stops her. "Nice to meet you, Boris! Come on, Mom. We have to get to Valdez!"

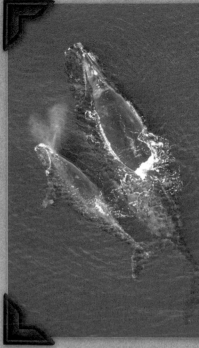

Bowhead Whale

Alaska's state **marine mammal** is the bowhead whale. This whale has a large, bony **skull**. It uses the top of its skull to break thick ice when it needs to breathe! A bowhead whale can be 66 feet (20 m) long. It has the largest mouth of any animal!

Gates of the Arctic National Park and Preserve

Gates of the Arctic National Park is north of the Arctic Circle! It has a lot of mountains, including the Brooks Range. There are no roads, trails, visitor centers, or campgrounds in the park.

Now Miranda is confused. "Monty, what about your ice pick?"

"I'll borrow one," Monty says. "It will be, you know, as easy as Eskimo pie!"

Miranda is very proud of her son. They return to the plane and fly to the Gates of the Arctic National Park. Miranda wants to show Monty the Brooks Range from the air.

Then they turn south and fly over Mount McKinley. It is the highest mountain in North America. "Maybe you can climb that mountain someday!" Miranda says. "We're almost to Valdez. You'll be climbing in no time."

"All right!" Monty says. "I can't wait to tell Morrie and Coco that my mom knows how to fly!"

THE END

Valdez

Valdez is a port city on Prince William Sound. In 1989, an oil tanker spilled more than ten million gallons of oil into the water. It was the largest oil spill in North American history.

Alaska at a Glance

Abbreviation: AK

Capital: Juneau

Largest city: Anchorage

Statehood: January 3, 1959 (49th state)

Area: 663,268 square miles (1,717,854 sq km) (the largest state)

Nickname: The Last Frontier or Land of the Midnight Sun

Motto: North to the Future

State flower: forget-me-not

State tree: Sitka spruce

State bird: willow ptarmigan

State fish: king salmon

State land mammal: moose

State marine mammal: bowhead whale

State insect: four-spot skimmer dragonfly

State song: "Alaska's Flag"

STATE SEAL

STATE QUARTER

The Alaska quarter shows a grizzly bear holding a salmon in its mouth. The grizzly and salmon symbolize Alaska's natural beauty and wildlife. The coin also has the North Star and the phrase, "The Great Land."

STATE FLAG

WHAT DO YOU KNOW?

How well do you remember the story? Match the pictures to the questions below! Then check your answers at the bottom of the page!

a. bush plane

b. bowhead whale

c. willow ptarmigan

d. sled dog race

e. Mount McKinley

f. frozen waterfalls

1. What do Monty and his friends like to climb?

2. What kind of animal is the park ranger?

3. What event is starting in Anchorage?

4. How do Monty and his mom get to Nome?

5. What kind of animal does Monty meet at the Bering Sea?

6. What do Miranda and Monty fly over on the way to Valdez?

What to Do in Alaska

1 **SEE TLINGIT TOTEM POLES**
Icy Strait Point, Hoonah

2 **RIDE A TRAIN THROUGH THE MOUNTAINS**
White Pass & Yukon Route Railway, Skagway

3 **LEARN ABOUT INUIT TOOLS**
Ulu Knife Factory, Anchorage

4 **CATCH SALMON ON THE KENAI RIVER**
Sprucewood Lodge, Soldotna

5 **WATCH KODIAK BEARS**
Kodiak, Kodiak Island

6 **VISIT THE VALLEY OF 10,000 SMOKES**
Katmai National Park and Preserve, King Salmon

7 **SEE THE NORTHERN LIGHTS**
Aurora Borealis Lodge, Fairbanks

8 **ATTEND AN INUPIAQ ESKIMO BLANKET TOSS**
Nalukataq Whaling Festival, Barrow

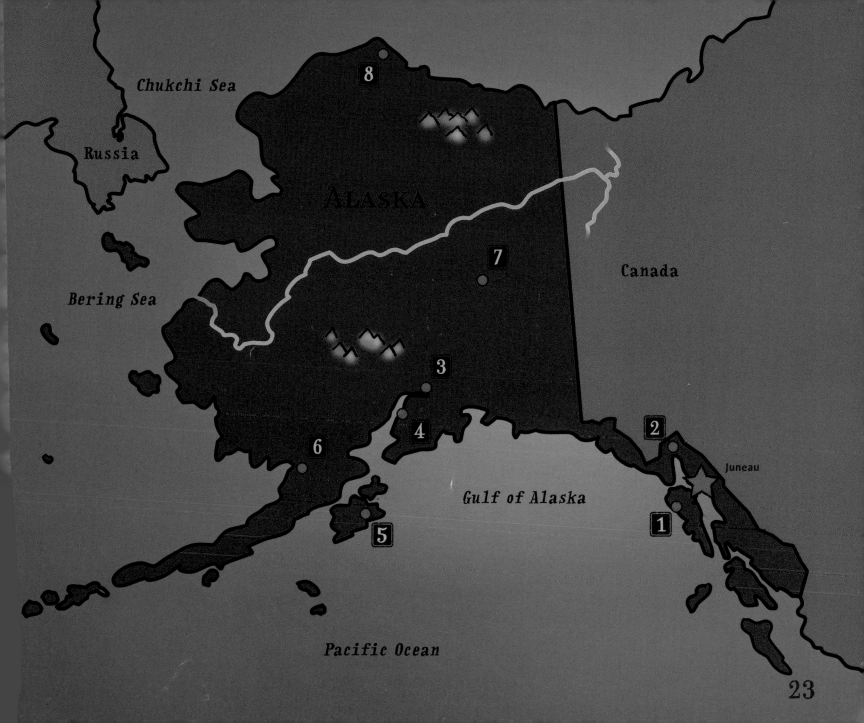

Chukchi Sea

Russia

Bering Sea

ALASKA

8

7

3

4

6

5

1

2

Juneau

Canada

Gulf of Alaska

Pacific Ocean

GLOSSARY

amazed – feeling surprised or full of wonder.

dangerous – able or likely to cause harm or injury.

describe – to tell about something with words or pictures.

mammal – a warm-blooded animal that has hair and whose females produce milk to feed their young.

marine – having to do with the sea.

medium-sized – not the largest or the smallest.

migrate – to move from one area to another, usually at about the same time each year.

panhandle – a narrow strip of land that is part of a larger area, such as a state or country.

prospector – a person who searches the land for oil or metals such as gold or silver.

shed – to lose something, such as skin, antlers, or fur, through a natural process.

skull – the bones that protect the brain and form the face.

24

About SUPER SANDCASTLE™

Bigger Books for Emerging Readers
Grades K–4

Created for library, classroom, and at-home use, Super SandCastle™ books support and engage young readers as they develop and build literacy skills and will increase their general knowledge about the world around them. Super SandCastle™ books are part of SandCastle™, the leading PreK–3 imprint for emerging and beginning readers. Super SandCastle™ features a larger trim size for more reading fun.

Let Us Know

Super SandCastle™ would like to hear your stories about reading this book. What was your favorite page? Was there something hard that you needed help with? Share the ups and downs of learning to read. We want to hear from you! Send us an e-mail.

sandcastle@abdopublishing.com

Contact us for a complete list of SandCastle™, Super SandCastle™, and other nonfiction and fiction titles from ABDO Publishing Company.

www.abdopublishing.com • 8000 West 78th Street
Edina, MN 55439 • 800-800-1312 • 952-831-1632 fax